HOME

The Residential Architecture of

D. Stanley Dixon

HOME

FOREWORD BY CHARLOTTE MOSS

RIZZOLI
NEW YORK

New York · Paris · London · Milan

To my mom and dad, Earline and Don,
for your unwavering support. You taught me the
value of hard work, nurtured my love
of houses, and, most importantly, informed my
knowledge of what home truly means.

CONTENTS

FOREWORD BY CHARLOTTE MOSS

BUILDING A HOUSE oftentimes begins with a dream. But how to get there, how to realize that dream, these are the questions we ask ourselves. Who will translate our ideas, put them to paper, and see us through the process to our new front door?

Several years ago, I attended a conference in Dublin with architect Stan Dixon and interior designer Suzanne Tucker. Afterward, the three of us decided to visit Northern Ireland. Three curious, kindred spirits, we explored classic, iconic, and royal residences together, savoring every last detail. It was on that trip that I thought to myself, "If and when I ever build another house for myself and my family, Stan will be my first call."

Today we are in the midst of our project together in Virginia. I was reluctant to place that first call as our home would be a renovation with "some additions," and I feared this would be a project not wholly representative of D. Stanley Dixon Architect. Thank God, I was wrong. Two years later we have doubled the square footage, limewashed the 1938 stone structure, created a tower so I can see the mountains, and added a rill off the terraces for music in the garden.

Our lives are often like equations summing up their parts. In Stan's case, his aesthetic, refined sensibility and penchant for classicism were informed by his birthplace in Tennessee, a mother who is an interior decorator, and the place he now calls home in Georgia. Irrespective of geography, all of these qualities combined with local influences are the foundation of each and every project. To intuit the heart of a house, to imbue it with history, poetry, and romance is an acquired skill set and one that Stan employs to navigate and guide us through the process.

Great taste, a discriminating and informed eye, curiosity, and a polite sense of humor are the makings of a great collaborative partner. Stan Dixon is all of that. A gentleman and a great listener, Stan hears what is being said and what is not said. The words being thought but not yet formed are drawn out of you as if by some hidden divining rod.

We study history, we commit it to memory, but understanding how to use it as a catalytic influence in one's life and work as a source of inspiration and its application is an enviable trait. Working within a traditional and classical framework, the skill of Stan's firm is its ability to coax the past to accept all of the requirements of life today. To anticipate the needs of the future, and to successfully marry traditional styles with modern demands and practicality.

Stan understands that the springboard for a dialogue with a client is one that begins with a dream. As that conversation expands, visualization starts to take place—floor plans, materials, whatever the imagination summons now begins to have flesh, so to speak, and a pencil begins to sketch a facade, a roofline, a fireplace, a floor pattern. Houses are great opportunities to tell our stories. It is incumbent upon an architect to help erase the inhibitions and fears and to inspire, excite, and guide us through the realm of possibilities.

But, back to the dream . . . In *The Poetics of Space*, Gaston Bachelard wrote, "the house shelters daydreaming, the house protects the dreamer, the house allows one to dream in peace." I am confident that the owners of the houses that follow here had their dreams interpreted, and each one will leave you wanting to know more about them.

Read on.

INTRODUCTION

I GREW UP IN Sumner County, Tennessee, along the Cumberland River on a bucolic property called Riverwood Farm that has been in my mother's family for five generations. My grandparents lived in what we called the homeplace, a simple Greek Revival structure built in the mid-1800s where they raised nine children and farmed the land. My parents, sister, and I lived in a different house on the same property. When he wasn't busy farming or being a father, my grandfather was a noteworthy county judge with a deep love for his community. I spent almost every day of my childhood at the homeplace drinking sweet tea on the swing with my grandmother. There was a magic to that house that has always remained with me.

My mother always had a passion for interior decorating; although she was never formally trained as a designer, she had an impeccable eye. She taught me about the important role of aesthetics in creating warm and inviting spaces. My father's side of the family contained a long line of builders, including my great uncle, who would salvage building materials from old houses in the area. As a young child I remember exploring the warehouses and barns he had filled with mantels, light fixtures, stained glass windows, bathtubs, wall paneling, moldings, and so on. I was mesmerized by the possibilities of what might become of these reclaimed objects.

Many of my family members on both sides lived in historic homes around rural Tennessee. One of my favorites was Elmwood, my aunt's historic Italianate house, where we sometimes gathered for family reunions. I loved the romance of the peacocks roaming her lawn; sipping lemonade on the brick terrace; sliding down curved wood banisters; and playing hide-and-seek with my cousins among the antiques.

All of this exposure from a young age gently nudged me to a place where I grew to admire everything about architecture, design, interiors, and gardens. I was drawn to the authenticity of materials, the process of a home's construction, and the timeless quality of design—all attributes I strive for in my work today. The subtle differences between eccentric, quirky, formal, and informal houses alike sparked my interest; but, most of all, I felt the grace and hospitality extended from the people who lived in these homes.

As I grew older these curiosities and passions continued to develop. I spent hours at the local bookstore flipping through collections of floor plans and renderings of old buildings. Eventually, the only presents I wanted for Christmases and birthdays were books about houses, magazine subscriptions, and a drawing board. With my father's old T square from college, I took drafting paper and tape and started sketching houses on the weekends. The entire story of a house and the people who lived there went from my imagination onto the paper. I often devised very elaborate story lines about the fictional homeowners, down to the car they would park in the motor court. Some afternoons I went down to the sandy banks of the shore and used a stick to draw plans of entire communities along the water's edge, imagining the views, topography, and natural vegetation of the landscape.

When I was in middle school, my parents built a new house and allowed me to participate in the process. I attended the design meetings and listened to my parents explain to the architect what they did and didn't like. I offered significant ideas and input about everything from the look and style of the front elevation to the layout of the rooms. My parents not only listened to my opinions, but valued them. This brought me a new sense of confidence, and the entire experience is something I am extremely grateful for.

By the time I entered college, pursuing a degree in architecture was the natural choice, and I savored every moment of it. I graduated from the University of Tennessee, receiving an amazing education with a focus on contemporary design and commercial architecture—an aesthetic I was drawn to at that point in my life. This approach to design, in conjunction with my early exposure to traditional southern residences, created a unique dichotomy that gives my work nuance.

After college, I moved to Atlanta to begin my career and before long I married my wife, Shannon, an interior designer who shares my passion for creating beautiful and hospitable houses. Watching her create a home for our family was transformative to my work. The experiences we shared renovating, decorating, and gardening together brought me great insight into the importance not only of beauty, but also modern functionality in a house. My wife's impeccable taste and talent continue to serve as a cornerstone in everything I do.

After working for several Atlanta-based residential firms, and a commercial design firm for five more years, I found my true calling working under renowned architect Norman Davenport Askins. It was a full circle moment, and I was finally given the opportunity to design the type of houses I had fantasized about as a child. Norman's discernment and faculty when it came to architecture was infectious, but I was particularly enamored by Norman's humor and charm. He possessed an innate ability to understand and value his clients and their needs and collaborate effectively with the entire design team.

Working alongside skilled interior designers, landscape architects, and tasteful creators broadened my horizons in ways I never could have imagined. Norman encouraged me to follow in his footsteps by continuing my education at the Attingham Trust in England. The on-site courses I took in architectural history and the heritage of British country houses had a profound influence. I was struck by the similarities between the ancient European homes I was studying and the southern homes I had grown up with. There were similarities not only in their looks, but in the way the houses felt. The views, the architecture, the way the structures interacted with the land, and the purposefulness of fulfilling a certain way of life were familiar sensibilities. These were houses that lived and breathed.

In 2006 I started my firm, D. Stanley Dixon Architect, in Atlanta, Georgia. Over the years, I have had the privilege to work on projects all over the country, some of which you will see in this book. Of course, we design these homes within the demands of today's modern lifestyle, but I believe they still resonate with the soulful romance and warmth of the past. From city to country, beach to mountain, every project has been a gift. It has been my good fortune to have wonderful and thoughtful clients who allow us to explore and create in such a variety of styles. Recalling my childhood, I continue to find joy in the beauty, authenticity, craft, and design of homes. From classic to contemporary, or a blend of the two, we strive to reflect the personal passions of those who call these buildings home.

—D.S.D.

CHAPTER 1

Neoclassical Elegance

PREVIOUS PAGE: In the foyer, the brass-and-iron staircase features balusters that we designed with a stylized bamboo motif.
ABOVE: The facade was inspired by a house built in the 1920s, adapted for this site; our interior floor plan is original. OPPOSITE: Shutters on the porch frame a peek into the hidden front courtyard. We designed the chair, one of a pair, flanking the front door. Landscape architect John Howard designed the terraced lawn and gardens.

SINCE STUDYING in Poland with my architecture professor, world travel has been integral to my process. On my journeys, I compulsively snap pictures of the details I encounter—the swept pine floors of a Swedish palace, the turned-wood fretwork of a Moroccan riad—as references for future projects. And while the influence my travels have had on my work is undeniable, the place that inspires me most is the city where I live: Atlanta, Georgia.

Atlanta's splendid neighborhoods are populated by an astounding variety of beautiful, historically significant homes designed by legendary architects such as Neel Reid, Philip Trammell Shutze, Leila Ross Wilburn, and James Means, as well as the firms of Pringle and Smith and Ivey and Crook. Their legacies have inspired generations of architects across the country, including myself.

This local project presented us with the perfect circumstance to put that inspiration to work. Our clients had lived on this terraced lot in an established tree-canopied neighborhood for more than twenty years. Now empty nesters, they recognized that the style of home they desired had shifted along with their needs and lifestyle. Initially, they considered renovating, but soon realized that they would not get the house of their dreams within the limitations of the existing structure and site. Their love of place remained strong and, in the end, they decided to begin anew on the property they called home.

Our primary source of inspiration was a 1921 Neel Reid–designed residence located in historic Ansley Park. This neoclassical home, while not grand in scale, remains exacting in its proportions, emanating an undeniably stately presence from its modest, hilltop perch. Its whitewashed brick exterior, rhythmic French doors, and pedimented entry were all seminal references in our design.

Recalling Reid's composition, we mirrored the facade to respond more comfortably to our client's property. Certain key features were modified: the symmetrical elevation was offset by an asymmetrical entry on the left side of the house, setting the tone for unexpected interior spaces to unfold. We amplified the scale of the structure to suit the clients' needs. Creating a natural flow from the public, entertaining spaces to the more personal, utilitarian spaces was of paramount concern to us. We carefully sequenced an array of materials, hardware, and moldings to function as a subliminal guide through the varied rooms. Formal areas received Federal-style moldings, refined brass hardware, and wide-plank oak floors, while the more casual spaces were outfitted with minimal moldings, rustic iron hardware, and irregular stone floors.

Throughout our conversations with the clients, we focused on conveying style without pretense. Despite the home's formal facade, the clients are unfussy people. They wanted their home to convey integrity and charm, with an easy and understated grace. We incorporated the husband's love of music into his private study by designing a custom steel-and-wood console to house his extensive record collection and sound system. We translated the wife's sentimental attachment to heirloom china, passed down through generations, into a charming, hidden butler's pantry adjacent to the dining room.

In a house like this, no one defining detail, focal point, or subtle gesture steals the show; the whole is far greater than the sum of its parts. By translating Atlanta's architectural dialect for a contemporary family, we breathed new life into southern elegance and eclecticism.

One of several, this door surround features a robust broken pediment and striking dentil molding detailing. A matching design in the living room creates an enfilade that draws the eye from one room to the next.

TREES

TREES

Interior designer Carolyn Malone was one of our longstanding collaborators on the house and was instrumental in having the architecture and interiors developed in tandem. The contemporary and eclectic furniture arrangement is conducive to easy living, and the space seamlessly blends formal architecture with casually elegant interiors that serve as the house's central hub.

ABOVE: One of the room's two cozy corner banquettes provides the perfect place to start the day. RIGHT: Three sets of towering French doors and windows allow sunlight to cascade across the room. In another nod to the 1920s, we designed thick walls for drapery pockets, which allow the curtains to recede when needed and the architecture detail around the openings to show.

OPPOSITE: A mix of family heirlooms and antiques paired with contemporary art and lighting in the dining room represents our clients' desire to combine various styles and eras for a uniquely personal design. ABOVE: A hidden jib door, one of a pair, leads to the butler's pantry. The two passages allow for easy flow into and out of the space. The doors practically disappear when closed.

We created an open-air environment in the butler's pantry so that many of the tabletop collections can be easily gathered at a glance. Most of the pieces are on display, instead of hidden behind cupboard doors, and can be enjoyed when not in use. We cataloged all of the clients' china, crystal, linens, and other serving pieces before we started allocating space for storage.

LEFT: Our clients love to cook, and the kitchen is often brimming with friends and family gathered around the island ready to assist—and the couple usually keeps a fire burning year-round. ABOVE: Portieres add softness and provide privacy without enclosing the space with doors. The brick wall and wood beam indicate a subliminal shift to rustic materials within the home's more casual spaces.

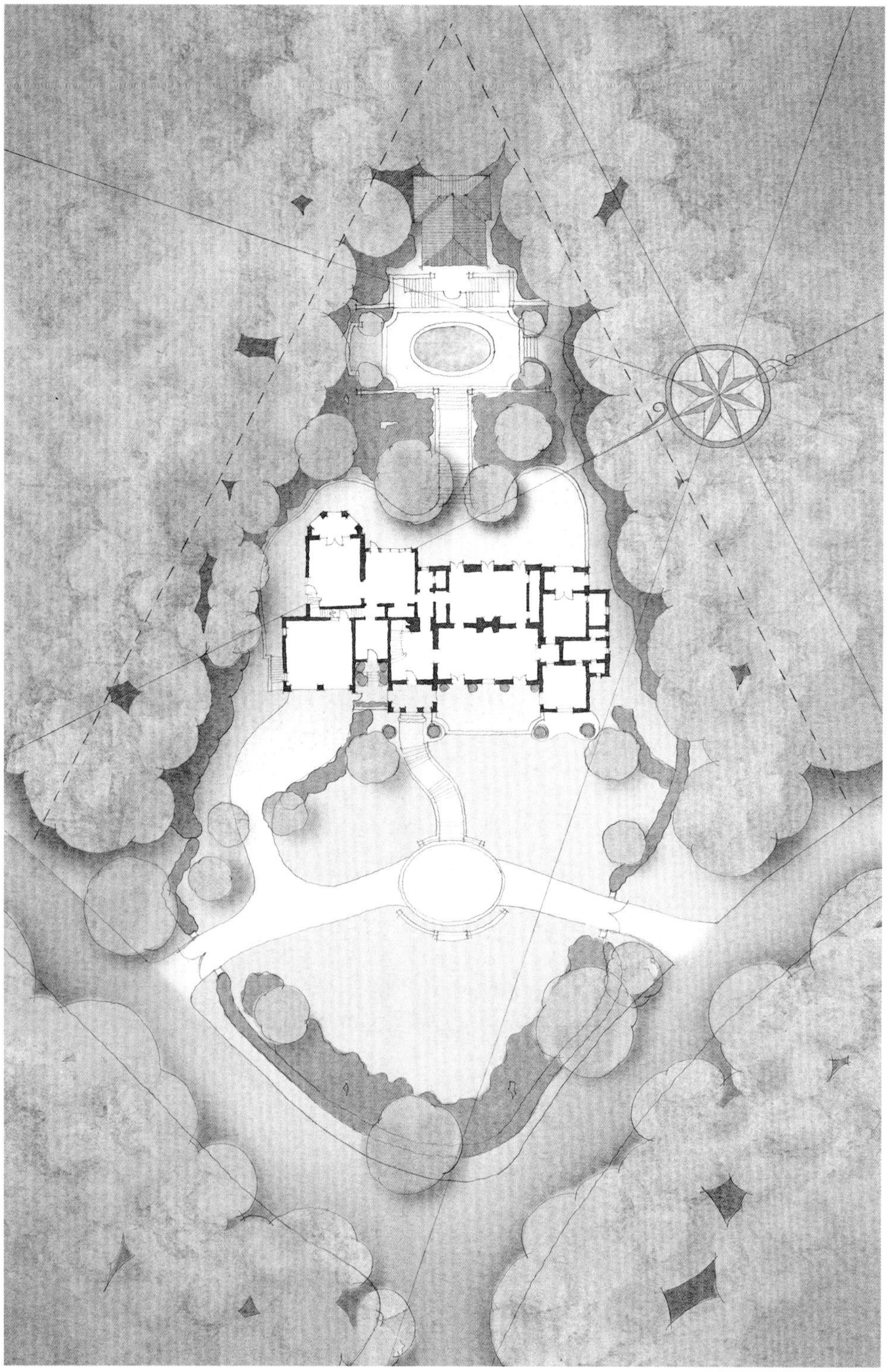

ABOVE: From the street, the pie-shaped lot gradually rises, with a pool and poolhouse at the pinnacle of the steep property. We echoed the shape of the pool by adding an elliptical motor court in front. OPPOSITE: Besides offering storage, the back entry's bespoke cabinetry camouflages an array of appliances, including a second oven, refrigerator, and wine cooler.

Our firm designed the bench in the family room, which was inspired by an antique from an English stable. Above it, a whimsical keyhole window lets sunlight spill into the enclosed back stairwell.

OPPOSITE: Pale-pink envelops the primary bedroom. Louvered shutters (far left) close over French doors to create more privacy, and the intimately scaled arched fireplace echoes the shape of the barrel-vaulted ceiling. ABOVE: A floating desk anchors the wife's study, which has access to the gravel-lined rear courtyard and gardens. An antiqued mirrored wall reflects light, shifting the room's mood throughout the day.

The husband is an avid music lover, and his study allows for both work as well as relaxing with his coveted album collection. Interior partition walls of wood and glass offer a level of privacy without completely closing the room off from other spaces.

CHAPTER 2

Vernacular Barn

LOCATED ON one of the highest plateaus in the Blue Ridge Mountains, with an elevation of nearly 3,500 feet, the storybook community of Cashiers, North Carolina, has long been a high-summer escape for fellow Southerners because of its inviting climate. The area offers a reprieve from the heat and humidity of its neighboring, more low-lying communities. Some days, you feel like you are floating in and above the clouds—because, in fact, you are. The clean, crisp mountain air immediately puts you at ease. The mountains, hills, and morning fog are transportive—mentally and physically. Our firm has designed numerous houses in the region, and I always welcome the opportunity to work on new projects there.

In a bucolic meadow with panoramic mountain views, we built a new residence based on the region's historic architectural vernacular and spellbinding arcadian landscape. Instead of looking to the area's residential structures for inspiration, we designed this house around the concept of a historic barn that had been converted into a home, and then expanded upon over time. The community is named after Gifford Pinchot, the first chief forester of the US Forest Service, who, along with Theodore Roosevelt, made conservation a national priority. We felt a responsibility to honor such a special location by designing a house informed by the principles of sustainability and environmental stewardship.

Barns and agricultural structures large and small dot the area's rolling landscape. They are so simplistic in their designs—stripped of almost any ornamentation—that

PREVIOUS PAGE: The exterior is typical of agricultural barns in the area, consisting of locally quarried stone, rough-sawn siding, and wood shingle roof. RIGHT: Outdoor terraces were kept minimal so that the rolling green lawn could be easily accessed within just a few steps of leaving the house.

they now convey a timeless, almost modernist sensibility. You can often see the original carpenter details at work. This dialect suited our past-meets-present storyline perfectly. Working within this narrative, our team began the extensive research process to find historically accurate details that could be adapted and incorporated into new, yet authentic, structures that pay homage to a bygone era.

The overscale barn doors pull back, revealing a wall of steel and glass, which opens to an entry and to provide a dramatic view through the house and out to the picture-perfect mountain view. The exterior is clad in vertically sawn cedar board, aged to a darker hue. One of the gables even features a wood bracket and pulley, which harkens to a time when hay would have been hoisted into the loft.

The open, loftlike interior plan reflects the form of a barn. The finishes are light and bright. The floors are reclaimed oak and the rough-hewn wood-clad walls and staircases are washed a lighter tone. The detailing—including the simply tapered newel posts—reference local fence posts.

A stone barnyard wall links the primary house to a viewing porch that looks to the mountains, designed as if it had been repurposed from an old shed. The dining room serves as a connector between these two structures. Exterior materials of stone and steel are used internally, to appear as if the space had been annexed and converted from a porch at some point in the past.

Experimenting with the concept of a structure evolving over time allows for the lines of style and period to be blurred, rules to be broken, and the creation of something original to materialize for yesterday, today, and tomorrow.

RIGHT: Framed by the door's entry, majestic mountain views lure you into the home. On the roof, a cupola allows light into the center of the house, while a pair of barnlike ventilators actually serve as the home's chimneys.

With its open risers, the staircase is evocative of the kind often found climbing to a barn loft.

LEFT: The wife collaborated with interior designer Barry Dixon on the furnishings and art placement. OVERLEAF: The open connection between the living room and kitchen allows for large gatherings in one central space. PAGE 48: Reclaimed character-grade oak floors, in random widths for a rustic aesthetic, cover most of the main level. PAGE 49: Multiple seating areas allow for intimate moments.

THE ART BOOK

PREVIOUS SPREAD: When closed, the service pantry door in the kitchen (at right), mimics the cabinetry and becomes a secret entrance. The cabinet on the left conceals the refrigerator. ABOVE AND OPPOSITE: For added character in the mudroom, we did not try to conceal the imperfections on the rough-sawn shiplap walls.

THEROUX

LEFT: The swimming pool was placed on an axis with the primary bedroom's glass doors, creating a reflecting-pool effect with the mountains. It's an ideal location for morning laps or late-night dips. OVERLEAF, LEFT: Typical throughout the house, a custom Z-braced barn door leads to the primary bath. OVERLEAF, RIGHT: The primary bath is wrapped in windows, and its walls are stained the same color as the exterior.

With its tall, rectangular niche for firewood storage and square firebox, the stone fireplace in the living room is its own graphic composition of interest. Clever design solutions for having easy access to firewood indoors are essential, as winters in the area can be cold and damp, and building fires a favorite pastime.

With its panoramic views, casual seating, and easy access to the outdoors, the dining room is a favorite spot for gathering. Glass-and-steel windows blur the lines between indoors and out, as do the floors in gray Crab Orchard stone, also used on the exterior.

ABOVE: After winding through the North Carolina forest, guests approach the house by crossing a cattle guard before entering the gravel court. The sound and vibration of driving over the threshold are subtle sensual cues that complement the house's agriculturally inspired aesthetic. RIGHT: The outdoor pavilion off the dining room, with its stone fireplace, is a natural spot for lounging.

CHAPTER 3

English Estate

THE GRACE and elegance of 1920s revival-style homes have always appealed to me. I was delighted when a young family approached me to build an English Tudor Revival manor in Atlanta. There would be a certain formality to the residence, as the style naturally lends itself to; however, their active lifestyle demanded that the house should function for modern living. We wanted to achieve elegance without stuffiness. It was also important to us that the house not be dark and moody, as historic homes of similar style tend to be.

The neighborhood off Tuxedo Park is filled with a mix of beautiful and charming Georgian, Federal, and English Revival residences. Our goal was to make the exterior feel original to the area. The couple wanted a stone house, so we chose a locally sourced, hand-chiseled Lithonia granite. The undulating surfaces of the stone give the house a softness and sense of permanence.

Sited on an expansive hilltop parcel, we had the luxury of expanding the home in multiple directions across the landscape. The unusual footprint allowed light to fill each room from multiple directions, captured spectacular views to the expansive gardens, and created interesting and defined exterior spaces.

The dramatic carved limestone door surround is one of the home's most significant and classical elements, referencing the work of legendary architects such as Sir Edwin Lutyens; Mellor, Meigs & Howe; and Harrie T. Lindeberg. The entry communicates the scale, splendor, and dignity of the house. Flanked by two equally powerful iron stanchions with gas lanterns that flicker around the clock, the entrance lends a sense of hospitality to the grand facade. Three majestic chimneys feature stone and handmade brick. The tall timber windows, made in France, include lead caming that create beautiful shadows as light dances through the house.

Inside, a gallery serves as a spine connecting the rooms on the main level—from the private quarters to a side-entry porch, a format typical of many 1920s homes. This gallery is not only beautiful but functional as a thoroughfare.

The mood evolves as one moves from public to private spaces. The formal gallery, living room, and dining room feature refined classical details. In the family room and kitchen wing, however, we shifted to elements with more patina, such as rustic wood beams on the ceiling. In the bedrooms, we lowered the ceilings to create cozier, more intimate environments.

The back lawn features a series of formal and informal outdoor spaces, including a loggia tucked against a stone wall overlooking a swimming pool. From the family room a handcrafted timber porch assembled with mortise-and-tenon joinery (as was done in the 1800s) has a strong sense of authenticity and craft. A similarly fabricated teahouse topped with a thatched roof is the focal point of the great lawn.

Local materials carefully pieced together by talented collaborators brought life to this house, proving again what a vital role time-honored craftsmanship plays in creating original, bespoke architecture.

PAGE 65: Guests pass a double-story bay window on the way to the front door. PREVIOUS SPREAD: While the house features a symmetrical core surrounding the front entrance, the footprint becomes asymmetrical as its wings expand in different directions, creating an unexpected, yet uniquely balanced composition. OPPOSITE: Custom stanchions with English-style gas lanterns flank the Indiana limestone entry surround with rusticated pilasters and pulvinated frieze.

ABOVE: The cantilevered wood treads of the staircase were inspired by similar ones, albeit in stone, from historic English country houses. The balustrade is brass and iron, and the handrail is ebonized mahogany. OPPOSITE: In the main gallery, the ceiling detailing matches the pattern of the limestone floor.

RIGHT: Our firm designed the Georgian-style, multicolored marble mantel in the living room. Light coming from the tall, elegant windows is reflected off the lacquered ceiling. Interior designer Suzanne Kasler was our collaborator on the project; together, we worked to ensure that all the rooms had an ethereal quality. OVERLEAF: An antique Jacobean-style oak mantel inspired the finish and detailing of the entire library, especially the crown molding. Oak paneling was bleached to keep the room light, yet it retains a sense of warmth. The ceiling detail was inspired by a Sir Edwin Lutyens design.

BUNNIES

OPPOSITE AND ABOVE: Surrounded by an elegant hand-painted floral wallpaper, the dining room opens to a lush walled courtyard garden, one of a series of intimate and expansive outdoor areas.

ABOVE AND RIGHT: Evocative of utilitarian spaces in English country houses, rustic plaster walls and reclaimed pine beams in the kitchen indicate a shift from the house's formal spaces.

THE FAMILY HOME

LEFT AND ABOVE: From watching TV to reading to playing games, the family room is truly the hub for daily activities. The doors flanking the fireplace lead to an outdoor living area that is the same size and scale as the family room. OVERLEAF: The primary bedroom is a cocoon-like retreat with drapery, walls, and headboard all swathed in silk. The sliding screen elegantly conceals a TV.

LEFT: In the wife's glamorous bathroom, we treated the marble as we often do wood paneling in a room. The space features dazzling Calacatta Violetta marble-clad walls with remarkable veining. Mirrored insets cleverly conceal storage. ABOVE: As a special touch to the vanity that we designed in her dressing area, we included a petite built-in sink.

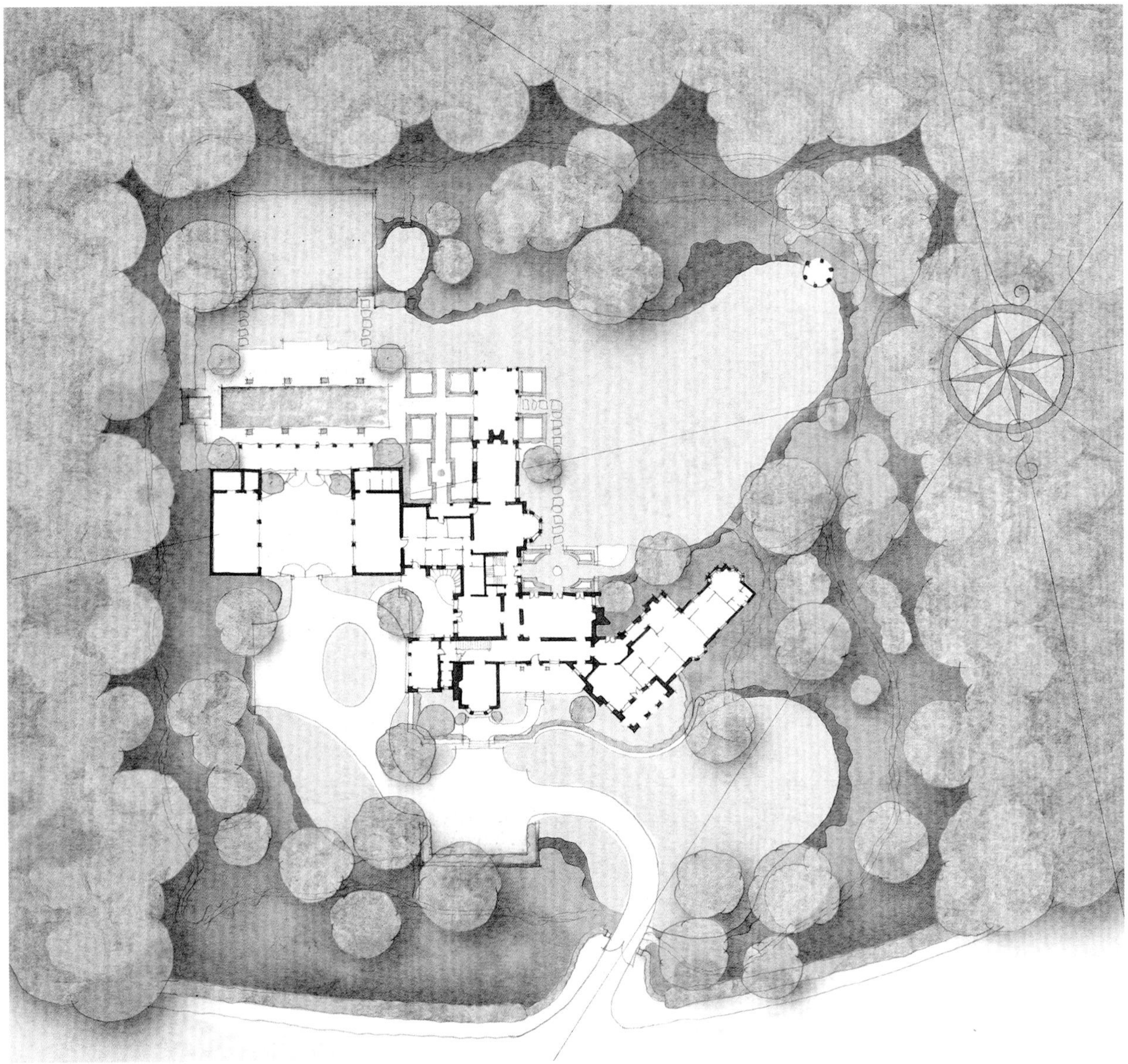

ABOVE: Many of the house's rooms have multiple exposures and access to the outdoors, a result of the generous lot size and ability to expand in various directions. The west side of the property features a private motor court flanked by a pair of carriage houses. Behind it is an entertaining loggia and Olympic-size swimming pool. OPPOSITE: The husband's study includes its own private porch.

LEFT AND OVERLEAF: Landscape architect John Howard was our collaborator on the garden design, which features a mix of landscaped terraces for entertaining, walled courtyard gardens, clipped boxwood hedges, and a lush lawn, as well as casual areas such as the loggia and pool area.

CHAPTER 4

Tropical Oasis

IN ARCHITECTURE, mystery can be a powerful tool—creating memorable spaces and eliciting memorable emotions. This house we designed on Jupiter Island, off the Atlantic coast of Florida, provides a wonderful example. You experience it long before you even lay eyes on it. A long, serpentine driveway—flanked by lush and mature sea grapes, royal palms, and ficus hedges—keeps guests from seeing too far ahead as it twists and bends. They arrive in a gravel courtyard, surprised to find a relatively demure facade that defies any distinct categorization, yet encourages curiosity for what lies beyond. The approach is a feast for the senses: the scent of brine and misty salt spray from the ocean waves in the distance, the crunch of pea gravel underfoot and the rustle of tropical foliage in the wind. These subtle gestures sweep you away.

My client, with whom I had collaborated previously on her primary residence in Atlanta, grew up spending her winters on this island. Those fond memories drew her to create an escape here for her young family. She purchased a 1970s ranch-style home on two acres of the same coast she collected seashells on as a child. With her primary home being a bit more formal, she wanted something carefree—but still elegant—and a place to express her love of unabashed color and pattern.

The original layout was a rambling, one-story plan with a weathered wood-clad exterior, cypress walls, and terrazzo floors that were pleasantly cool to bare feet—Old Florida touchstones that both the client and I loved. She astutely lived in the house for a couple of winter seasons to get a better understanding of the space before embarking on the renovation, which eventually became a complete transformation. Collectively, we thought about what the house could be and conclusively landed on a vernacular that draws inspiration from coastal locations around the world, including Bermuda, Greece, and Morocco. The mélange of architectural details includes stepped ziggurats, scalloped gables, extensive courtyards and loggias, and even Chippendale fretwork screens evocative of British colonial design. The consistency of materials and color allowed the disparate shapes and forms to work in unison.

Once inside the louvered entrance, a large exterior pavilion takes the place of a traditional foyer. A long outdoor passageway connects the main house to the pool house—surrounded by a lush courtyard, which becomes an extension of the house, designed for entertaining and gathering. A loggia guides you to the entrance hall, which frames postcard-worthy views of the beach. The various wings of the house allow us to produce a series of intimate conversation and lounging areas. Even when the house is full of guests, there's always a cozy spot where one can steal away for a bit of privacy. The interior design of the house maintains the Old Florida feel with black terrazzo floors and limewashed cypress walls. Colorful art and fabrics promote a joyful and playful atmosphere. Inside and out, the eclectic styles of island architecture and interiors prevail to create a timeless sense of relaxation, happiness, and ease.

There is a nostalgic quality to this home. Its mystery and eclectic beauty harken back to the imaginative and playful naïveté of childhood. The owner captured this sentiment perfectly when naming the property Tres Besitos, an homage to her three children.

PAGE 93: A stepped ziggurat roof reminiscent of a Bermudan buttery caps the entry pavilion. PREVIOUS SPREAD: The house is adorned with a series of fanciful, scalloped gables and large, ocean-facing windows. OPPOSITE: Our firm designed the entry's Moroccan-inspired lanterns. The open-air pavilion functions as a de facto foyer.

PREVIOUS SPREAD: The house's indoors and outdoors were created as a whole—nothing was designed for either space without considering the effect on the other. When the living room's sliding pocket doors disappear, the lawn becomes an extension of the space. RIGHT: The living room is the heart of the home. With walls of windows facing east and west, you can watch the sun rise over the Atlantic Ocean and set across the verdant lawn.

The entry hall encapsulates our client's love of glamour, color, and a bit of humor. Black terrazzo floors run throughout much of the house. Interior designer (and my wife) Shannon Dixon and I collaborated on the interiors.

The family starts every day with breakfast around the stainless steel kitchen island. The diagonal louvered doors and crenelated tops of the kitchen cabinets evoke fanciful design elements found throughout the Caribbean.

ABOVE: The site design makes the most of its direct connection to the Atlantic Ocean. Our rendering highlights how the loggia is the connective thread that unites the property. RIGHT: A vibrant guest bedroom filled with color, pattern, and texture exudes a fanciful yet welcoming spirit.

The shape of the primary bedroom's custom headboard emulates the forms of the scalloped gables on the exterior.

LEFT: The loggia hosts long lunches by the pool, afternoon naps, evening cocktails, and even perches for playing games. OVERLEAF: The pool's water features produce a resplendent, relaxing sound that wafts across the property. PAGES 114-115: The residence acts as a barrier to the Atlantic, protecting the pool and courtyard from the wind and salty air. Activities and gatherings often spill down the terraced lawn.

CHAPTER 5

Edited Style

PAGE 117 AND PREVIOUS SPREAD: Most of the house is fitted with elegant glass-and-steel windows and doors painted in a soft French gray. It features a graduated Vermont slate roof in shades of tan, green-gray, and a hint of lavender. Our firm designed the gas lantern over the open-air portico. ABOVE: Custom burnished bronze hardware adorns paneled doors made of French oak. OPPOSITE: Reflective plaster walls create a luminous effect in the stairwell.

INSPIRATION CAN COME in many forms. In this case, it was a tiny two-inch image of historic stone and stucco farm buildings in Europe that my client brought to our first meeting for a new build in Atlanta. She had held onto this magazine clipping for years, waiting for the right time, and when she showed it to me I found myself equally drawn to it. There was strength in the simple forms and edited architecture. Nothing in the image was superfluous. We both loved the pure gabled roof geometry and the unique exterior spaces that developed as these structures sat among themselves. This single image jump-started our creative conversation for the house we built together, a downsize from the much larger and more formal French-style home where she and her husband had raised their children. Although they loved that home, the clients were looking for something simpler, both in aesthetic and function.

Restraint is something we often employ in our work to create harmony, and for this house a disciplined approach informed every decision—from the size of the house and the rooms within, to the materials we used. Even the decor is highly edited. Yet, while we took a less-is-more route, the house is still imbued with a warmth and soul that emanates from materials like stucco, plaster, antique French limestone, and rough-hewn timbers. Almost every room has access to the outdoors, including intimate, informal courtyards that act as extensions of the interior spaces. Although absent of any ornamentation, the proportions remain true to classical design, awarding timelessness to the architecture.

The clients didn't want the house to be too large; they only wanted to build rooms that would be used regularly, with no wasted space. The house is organized with the living room and an exterior courtyard as the symmetrical central core. The residence has few hallways, so these two central spaces are critical to the flow of the house. The rooms we pass through are often the rooms that we use the most. After progressing through the central hub, the bedroom and kitchen wings emerge—asymmetrical and more organic—giving way to function and relaxation. Axial views from one room to the next connect the spaces, gradually easing into more casual and flexible pathways in the house's more informal spaces.

One of the home's most purposeful features is the presence of sunlight from multiple directions in almost every room, resulting in a house that evolves throughout the day. You don't get high contrast of either wholly dark or light spaces because the light approaches from several angles at all times. We purposefully designed the living space only one room deep, with tall windows on both sides, for just this reason.

Inside and out, with its ever-changing shadows, the quiet, neutral palette projects a sense of peace and calm, allowing all of the elements to sit quietly in accord.

After moving in and living in the home some time, my client called me on the telephone to tell me how happy she was, and she gave me one of my favorite compliments: "It's so relaxing—I feel like I am on vacation every day!" In this moment, I knew we had achieved our goal. We had evoked the simplistic serenity of the old-world countryside in the picture.

Guests are greeted by a cozy, intimate foyer before the home's soaring, light-filled spaces reveal themselves.

Interior designer Carolyn Malone deftly composed a furniture plan that includes pieces in a range of styles, eras, and periods to meld seamlessly with the European-inflected architectural envelope. The antique stone fireplace, sourced from France, provides a fitting focal point.

French oak paneling creates a snug space that serves as a sitting room, TV room, and library.

Because of the extra-wide opening into the kitchen, we knew that we had to create something special for the clients to cast their gaze upon. A paneled island crafted from Carrara marble anchors the space in a monumental way. Not one to forgo form over function, we tucked counter seating at each end, so there is also space for dining, yet the backs of the stools are not the focal point when peering into the room.

OPPOSITE: The kitchen fireplace, a favorite of the clients, features an elevated hearth and storage underneath. ABOVE: All of the marble veining lines up seamlessly on the fronts of the island drawers, which provide ample storage in a kitchen without upper cabinets. There is also a pantry next to the open doorway.

OPPOSITE AND ABOVE: The primary bedroom features a bed that is sculptural, architectural, and graceful. It was created by designer Carolyn Malone and artist Raymond Goins. Whether the doors are closed or open, the room offers a direct view onto the rear terrace.

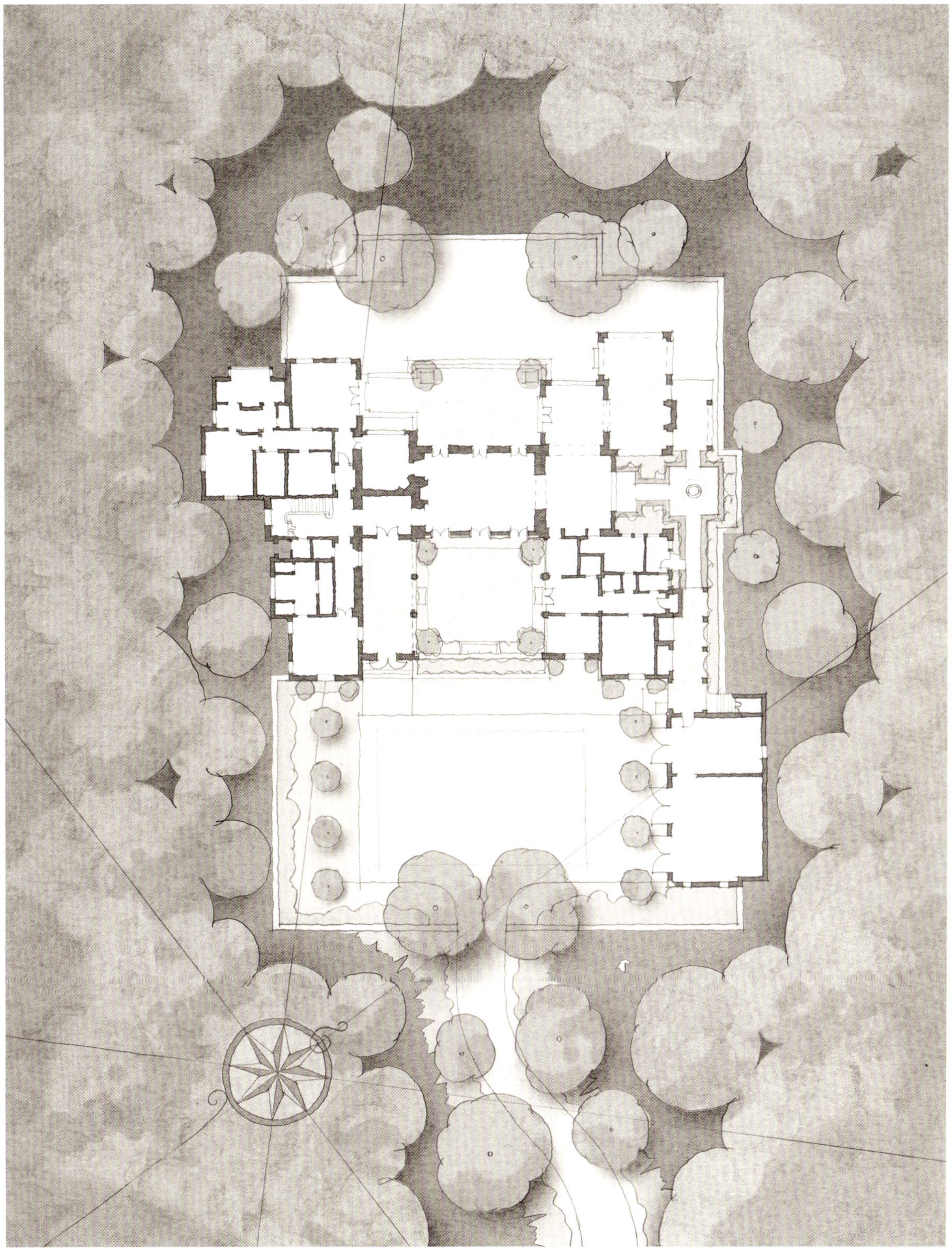

LEFT: An avid gardener, the wife was instrumental in designing the planting schemes, both with the front public-facing spaces and the surrounding private courtyards. ABOVE: The H-shaped site plan allows for courtyards both front and back—perfect for trickling fountains, stone terraces, and dining alfresco.

CHAPTER 6

Island Retreat

PAGE 137: Mixing formality with whimsy, we placed a swooping, scalloped lattice awning next to stately coquina quoins on the facade. PREVIOUS SPREAD: The glass-enclosed space is shaded by a canopy of grand oaks. A floating cantilevered staircase keeps pressure off the trees' roots. ABOVE: Turned wooden posts give the impression that an original porch had been converted into a sunroom. OPPOSITE: From the transoms and shutters to the signature hue, the late Oliver Messel's influence is evident upon arrival.

OPPOSITE: The open-air porch leads into the foyer, another space defined by a stylish nonchalance. For interest, we added a subtle dibbler detail around the ceiling. ABOVE: The louvered cabinets in the entry porch store everything from towels and tote bags to sunscreen and toys, making an impromptu trip to the pool or beach a cinch.

The living room's design by Kristin Blood, who was our collaborator on the entire house, contains essentials for island living: wicker and woven materials, coral accents, and plenty of room for the owners to host their children, grandchildren, extended family, and friends from near and afar.

LONG BEFORE setting pencil to paper for this client's new home on a barrier island off the coast of Georgia, we went to extraordinary lengths to examine, study, and assess in person the land on which we would be building. So many factors come into consideration when siting a home: what feels most appropriate to the surrounding environment; each room's orientation to natural light; how to frame the most beautiful vistas through the placement of windows, doorways, and other apertures. Watching how the sun moves throughout the day and casts shadows informs our design decisions so we can maximize the beauty nature has provided. For this piece of land, the most extraordinary site challenge was simultaneously its greatest asset: the more than one-hundred-year-old grand live oaks dripping with Spanish moss that swept across the property, with branches extending over forty feet from the trunks in all directions. With great respect, we designed a home that resides beneath and among these majestic branches. Although they presented a challenge, these trees became a defining attribute that gave scale, character, and a sense of place.

After spending years as seasonal visitors, our clients were ready to make Sea Island their full-time home. The couple was particularly inspired by the designs of Oliver Messel, the celebrated English aristocrat turned set designer turned Caribbean designer, as well as Addison Mizner, the Palm Beach architect who designed Sea Island's legendary resort, the Cloister. Following its construction in 1928, the Cloister inspired the architecture of surrounding areas for decades to come. We continued that legacy, layering Messel's design sensibilities with Mizner's Mediterranean and Spanish Revival architectural forms.

Known for melding traditional and tropical designs with an air of romance and folly, Messel had a flair for incorporating awnings, latticework, and other decorative woodwork, such as louvered shutters, into his designs. In his hands, these features were highly decorative, yet purposeful, allowing for courtyard doors and windows to be closed for privacy while allowing ever-important ocean winds to pass through. Among his signature design elements, perhaps the most notable and enduring is a unique shade of green widely known today as Messel Green. We used this color liberally throughout the project, grounding the house in historical distinction and flair.

Although we took inspiration from Messel's creativity and ingenuity, we didn't want to simply replicate his work in any way: that would be boring. We find it exciting to take inspiration from another place, another time, and bring it into the modern day. For instance, Messel generally preferred symmetrical structures. This house is anything but. In fact, it is rambling, playful, and at times whimsical, both in its design and finishes. The home feels expansive yet intimate, structured to take one on a melodic procession through interior and exterior living.

Above all, this house is rooted in its natural surroundings. The trees ruled over the design process more so than any personal taste or archival precedent. The contemporary yet historically informed structure appears as if the trees grew up around it, rather than vice versa. The resulting architecture exudes permanence and storied elegance.

Messel-inspired transoms top doorways leading into the sunroom. Gauzy curtains add structure, yet still allow sunlight to reach interior rooms.

On pleasant days without heat and humidity, the doors of the sunroom are opened to enjoy the weather. Full of light, the room is where the owners spend much of their time during the day.

OPPOSITE: The owners did not want a completely open floor plan, but when needed, pocketed lattice screen panels can be rolled out of sight or slid closed to provide privacy between the dining room and kitchen. ABOVE: The interior designer used the same pattern of the wallcovering on sheer curtain panels, which appear as light as air.

ABOVE: Mirror-backed latticework adds reflectivity and luminosity to the wet bar, a fully stocked area at the ready for both dinner parties or impromptu get-togethers. OPPOSITE: Large-scale windows in the kitchen frame postcard-worthy views into the lush semitropical landscape.

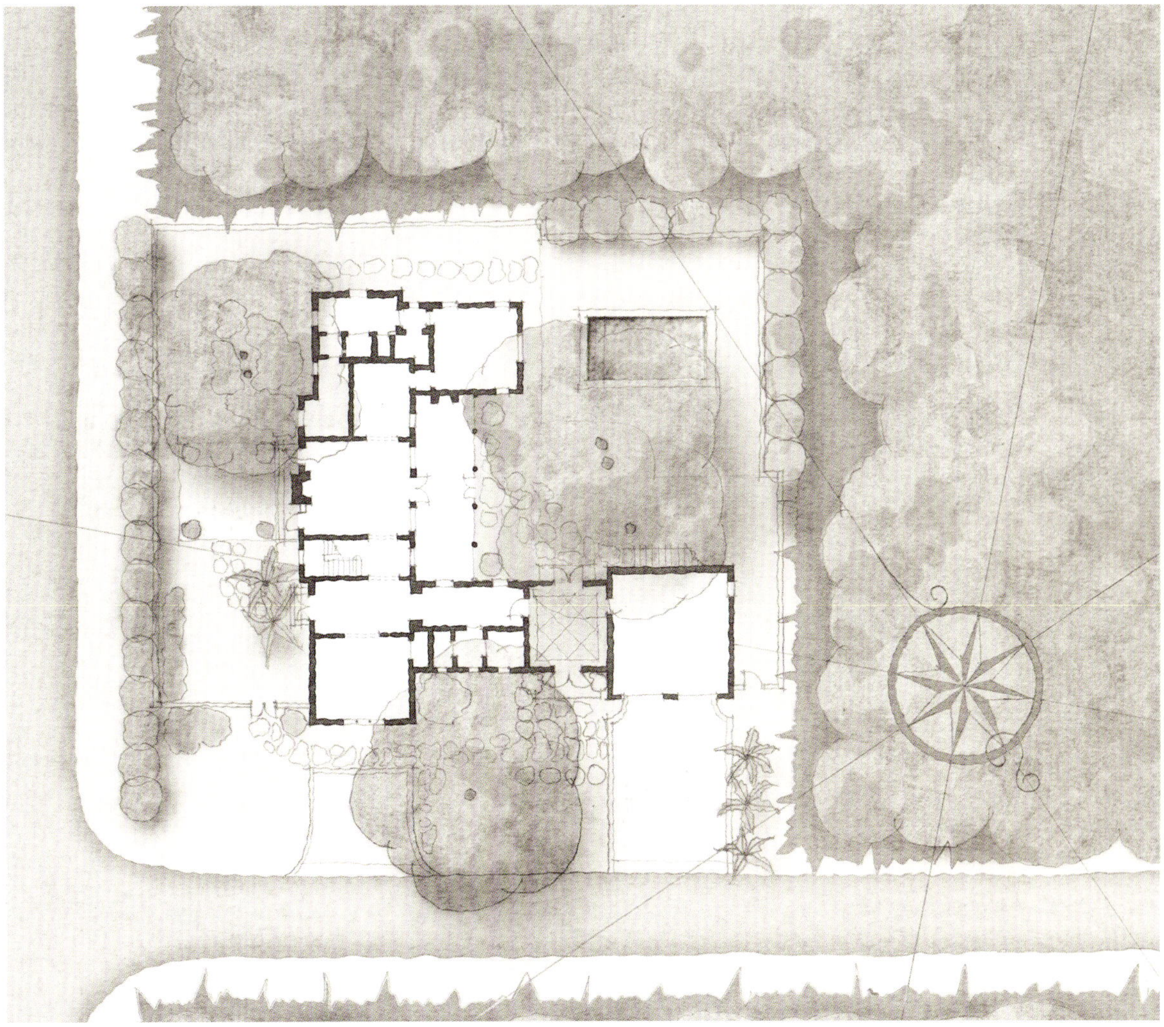

LEFT: Alfresco entertaining is de rigueur throughout most of the year. The home's understated stucco finish is the perfect foil to the vibrant green accents. ABOVE: We accounted for every branch on every tree that dictated the plan—and roof heights—for this house, which is located only half a block from the beach.

CHAPTER 7

Cotswold Manor

SOMETIMES a single detail can spark an entire house. In this case, it was a charming argyle-paneled door our client had stumbled across while reading an article about the Cotswolds region of England. She was drawn to the warm tones of the French oak as well as the functionality of the unique layered door system: an exterior set of doors with a wood frame and lead glass panels standing before a second set made of solid wood. The sturdier interior doors can be left closed at night for security and privacy and opened during the day to allow light to shine through. Our client had spent time in the Cotswolds during her youth, and the storybook style of the region had always spoken to her. We started our design process with the front entrance and worked our way outwards to create an English-inspired home suited for a distinguished residential neighborhood in Atlanta.

We originally consulted with the clients about restoring a pre-existing Tudor-style house in the area, but our feasibility reports determined the property, even with extensive renovations, would not suit their needs long-term. Fortunately, an empty lot became available that offered us the opportunity to build our clients their ideal home, with adequate space for extensive landscaping, gardens, and a pool. The depth of the property allowed us to place the house farther from the street, affording a precious sense of privacy and preserving many of the large, impressive trees that bordered the property. These trees became an important element in providing scale and maturity to our design.

We increased the size of the doorway in the reference to be proportionate with the larger house. The formidable entrance and symmetrical facade of handmade brick emanate a stately grandeur. A pair of monumental chimneys flank the entry—a unique composition reflective of English manors. Inside, we added robust millwork detailing, particularly to the ceilings, as a nod to the work of English architect Sir Edwin Lutyens. In the dining room, geometric circles and squares composed of heavy coffering provide interest to the space. We felt the expansive ceiling plane of the lengthy family room required interruption, so we introduced a series of beams at varying depths accompanied by egg and dart fretwork.

The house needed to reflect the vivacious spirit of the clients and their young family; the rooms possess a bright and airy feeling. The exaggerated proportions of the windows bring in abundant sunlight and accentuate the height of the ceilings. The back of the house opens generously to the pristine lawned courtyard and pool beyond where limestone voussoir arches create an arcade of indoor-outdoor living spaces. This highly disciplined and symmetrical composition maintains the strength of the architecture.

Our client's affinity for the English countryside is something we share, a sentiment I took with me from my time studying at the Attingham Trust as a young man. I greatly enjoyed applying the historical paradigm I learned as an architecture student in England to this timeless house in my hometown.

PAGE 157: A series of arched glass doors lead to the primary bedroom. Our firm created the bench with designer Jackye Lanham, who balanced the needs of an active, young family with the desire for beautifully tailored interiors. PREVIOUS SPREAD: Overscale chimneys create strength and balance. The roof is composed of a multicolored Vermont slate. OPPOSITE: The doors that inspired the home's design feature an argyle-paneled motif. The floors are French limestone embellished with black Belgian cabochons.

The family room spans the back of the house and is divided into two seating groups—it's as welcoming for two people as for twenty. The area in the foreground is the everyday gathering spot for relaxing or watching TV; when the family hosts larger parties, guests often settle near the fireplace or perch on one of the room's cozy built-in window seats.

the Potter's eye
Decorating Master Class

ABOVE: The owners regularly host friends for dinner and open their home for many charitable causes, so an elegant room for entertaining and dining was imperative for them. The ceiling was inspired by a historic English country house designed by Sir Edwin Lutyens. OPPOSITE: A carved limestone mantel, hand-painted wallpaper, and silk draperies are some of the room's elegant notes.

ABOVE: The family dining area is a bustling space, even when not in use for eating, and can be closed off from the kitchen as needed. RIGHT: The large French oak island was inspired by a series of round and rectangular tables I discovered while visiting Castle Drogo in England. We had this one fabricated locally. The elegant plaster range hood is flanked by windows that define each corner and open the room to the outdoors.

WOLF

ABOVE: Formality and symmetry define the site plan, from the front arrival court through the house and onto the back lawn flanked by two long arcades. RIGHT: Crafted from Kansas limestone, an arcade of voussoir arches define spaces both indoors and out.

The repetition of the arches adds a robust dimension to the architecture, including this loggia for entertaining. Across the lawn, a replica of the arcade houses the primary bedroom. Large-scale windows placed within each arch provide views of the verdant gardens designed by landscape architect John Howard.

CHAPTER 8

Lowcountry Charm

PREVIOUS PAGE: The house is sited on one of the Lowcountry's most secluded, idyllic islands. RIGHT: The front porch accommodates a number of activities beyond greeting guests. A custom cabinet (at right) conceals a commercial ice maker to fill coolers for a day on the water. The paneled door between the cabinet and entry leads to the laundry room. Behind a Dutch door (far left), a secondary kitchen is ready to accept the catch of the day.

ALTHOUGH OUR FIRM focuses predominantly on new builds, the projects we find most rewarding are the ones that grant us the opportunity to give significant, pre-existing homes a second life. That is what we achieved for this nineteenth-century cottage located in a village dating back to the late 1700s in the heart of South Carolina's storied Lowcountry. Rich biodiversity, regional cuisine, and unique local architecture define this area—made up of coastal waterways and salt marshes—on the tip of Wadmalaw Island.

The neighborhood remains miraculously untouched, undeveloped, and unspoiled. The houses lining the river retain their original, historic architectural features: white clap-board siding, painted metal roofs, sweeping wooden porches, and operable shutters. Over the years we have worked on many projects in the region, and the landscape provides a constant source of inspiration that we strive to honor and protect. Although it seems quite remote, the island is located only a short distance from Charleston, making it an easy weekend getaway.

Our clients, a couple from the city, purchased the house as a retreat for their family and friends. The original open, airy structure was simple and classic, originally designed for seamless indoor-outdoor living. Unfortunately, under a previous owner, the house had received a somewhat awkward and insensitive addition during the 1980s. Our goal was to respect the building's original charm and neighborly character by returning it to its former grace, while simultaneously connecting it with the present by adding a few modern updates, including a new kitchen, living area, and primary suite. In addition, the entire house had to be brought to level; naturally, over time, the floors had settled two inches out of plumb.

Returning the house to its period roots was an extensive process. An authentic porch was redesigned to wrap around the entire building with both open and enclosed portions, giving space for new bedrooms, bathrooms, and a pantry. All of the exterior wood cladding and interior walls were removed, restored, and refinished before being put back into place (there is almost no Sheetrock in the entire structure). Chimneys were rebuilt out of reclaimed handmade bricks, and the steep, somewhat dangerous main staircase was redesigned and reconstructed to meet modern building codes. We designed the primary suite as though it had originally been connected to the main house by a breezeway that, perhaps, had been enclosed at some point over the past two-hundred years. The hand-painted roof with its manually crimped standing seams feels as though it has withstood the test of time even though it's brand new.

On the old dirt roads that lead to this oasis, the only establishments for miles are a mom-and-pop grocery, a handful of churches, and a local sailing club that hosts weekend dances. The town's residents have kept the century-old traditions of sailboat regattas and oyster roasts alive and well. Spanish moss hangs from the gnarly limbs of ancient trees, and in the evenings the chirping sounds of cicadas against the quiet night sky recalls a bygone era. It's an honor to have restored and protected such a soulful narrative through our work.

There are no shortage of activities on the adjacent waterfront, including boating and fishing. The screened porch leads to the dock. We preserved the rustic texture of the ceiling boards. The diagonal wall boards had to be replaced and are new, but we replicated very closely what was existing before the renovation.

OPPOSITE AND ABOVE: A combination dining area and library is one of the home's coziest spaces. We designed the bookcases in a style we call carpenter chic. Anything more formal would have been antithetical to the house's simple, pure lines and uncomplicated methods of construction. We added doors to create direct access to the screened porch.

ACCIDENTALLY WES ANDERSON
THE FAMILY OF HUMMINGBIRDS

PAGES 180-181: Sensitive to not overpower the original two-story cottage, we were able to combine a new living room, dining area, and kitchen into one long, low-lying wing. PREVIOUS SPREAD: The kitchen features painted floors and countertops. Whimsical Gothic-arch detailing recalls a time when unique and decorative shapes were cut by carpenters from simple flat boards. RIGHT: Working with designer Jackye Lanham on the interiors, we outfitted this room as a bar area using antique furnishings instead of new built-ins. The arrangement of pieces complements the charm of the original architecture.

WHEATLEY VODKA

The Chief

LEFT: The primary bedroom features exposed rafters and a vaulted ceiling. ABOVE: A side-entry corridor, with a row of custom storage cabinets, is just outside the primary bedroom.

OPPOSITE: The water closet is separated from the rest of the bathroom by a board partition wall. Juxtaposing wide vertical with narrow horizontal boards adds simple, yet unexpected, visual interest for an often overlooked space. A working transom allows light to filter though. Painted wood floors add charm. ABOVE: Collections that have evolved over time are grouped and displayed.

During our design process, we imagined that the secondary kitchen had been renovated, perhaps, in the 1940s. Accordingly, we topped the cabinets with laminate countertops popular in the day and adorned them with a metal banding. Industrial-style hardware evocative of the era rounds out our inspiration.

LEFT: The screened porch marries the creature comforts of the indoors with the enduring pleasures of being in natural surroundings. ABOVE: The undelineated path to the house works with the simplicity and purity of the original architecture. OVERLEAF: The new addition on the right complements the original cottage.

CHAPTER 9

Coastal Arts and Crafts

NESTLED BETWEEN the ocean and sweeping coastal dunes on one side and a lovely grove of grand live oaks on the other, this English manor–style country house on the Atlantic coast feels as grounded and authentic here as it would in the British countryside. At first, this vocabulary may not be what you would associate with a private oceanfront property on a barrier island overlooking the South Carolina coast, but for these engaged, willing, and adventurous clients, that is exactly what we created: something conceptually incongruous, but absolutely ideal. The concept for this home was not totally without precedent. In the early 2000s, a golf club inspired by the rural English estates designed by architect C. F. A. Voysey was built on Kiawah Island, where this home is located. Since then, various residential interpretations of his work began popping up around the island.

Hallmarks of Voysey's designs include sweeping gabled and hipped roofs, ribbons of horizontal and vertical lead glass windows, canted buttresses, and stylistic elements of the arts and crafts and British art nouveau movements. We incorporated many similar design elements into this home, but where Voysey's homes generally featured slate roofs and white-stucco facades, we chose a flat clay-tile roof and a tabby-clad exterior to marry the house more appropriately to its regional, lowcountry location. Tabby is a form of concrete created by burning oyster shells to create lime, that is then mixed with water, sand, ash, and broken oyster shells. We went to great lengths to match the tabby to the exact color of wet beach sand nearby so that the house would blend seamlessly with the landscape.

In fact, we allowed the island's landscape, as well as the topography of the site, to guide the footprint of the house. With its oceanfront location, the first floor of the house needed to be elevated fourteen feet above natural grade to protect against floods and hurricanes. This made the structure much higher than its natural surroundings. One of the more challenging aspects of the project was to retain a human scale rather than a hulking structure that overpowered the site or its occupants. We accomplished this by creating a series of planters, stairs, and landings that grounded the home and guided one's progression to the front entrance in a natural and incidental manner.

Once across the threshold, one ascends the final few steps into the public rooms of the main floor (which are, in fact, located on the second floor). Inside, you are greeted by a sweeping view of the Atlantic Ocean. Simple materials create continuity from room to room. Stone floors seamlessly flow through the spaces. Light bounces off the highly reflective surfaces of Venetian plaster walls in gentle hues of wheat and sand. A limewash finish subtly enhances the rough-hewn texture of timber beams. Cypress-wood panels meet bronze hardware finishes to support the warmth of the home's palette. Through these richly varied moments, the individual elements come together in harmony.

There is a strength and formidable nature to this home, reminiscent of a Scottish manor on a windy coast: a warm and welcoming fortress where multiple generations gather together under a single roof—a bastion softened by subtle coastal influence. It's the unassuming components of this home—the meandering boardwalk, louvered breezeways, and trickling fountains—that prove themselves to have the most impact in the end.

PAGE 197: Venetian plaster walls reflect light in a dramatic arched corridor. PREVIOUS SPREAD: The facade of the English country house–inspired residence. OPPOSITE: A Voysey-inspired gate graces the carriage house.

The tucked-away front door (located behind the terracotta urn), is accessed via multiple terraces, stairways, and a trickling fountain.

ABOVE: Pecky cypress envelopes the intimate foyer. RIGHT: In contrast to the English-style lead glass windows on the front of the house, bronze windows with unifying proportions in the back allow for more expansive views of the Atlantic Ocean.

ABOVE AND RIGHT: The library is surrounded by dramatic cerused oak walls and includes a bar for easy entertaining.

Rothko Chapel
WILTON HOUSE

A combination family, dining, sitting room, and kitchen (overleaf) reflects the clients desire to have living areas that work just as well when they are there together or hosting family and friends. We collaborated with interior designer Beth Webb to imagine how individual spaces in the house can serve multiple purposes.

Interiors Atelier AM

The stair hall embraces a wealth of natural materials, including English York stone on the floors, pecky cypress and plaster on the walls, and rustic reclaimed beams on the ceiling.

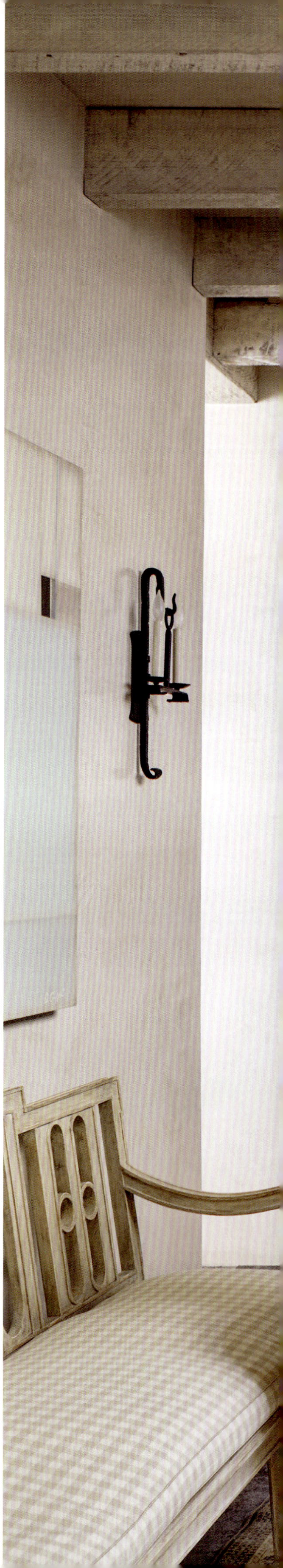

ABOVE: The primary bath is a sybaritic retreat that maximizes the ocean views. RIGHT: The angular lines of the primary bedroom echo the architectural ceiling structure, reminiscent of the childlike mystery of living amongst the eaves.

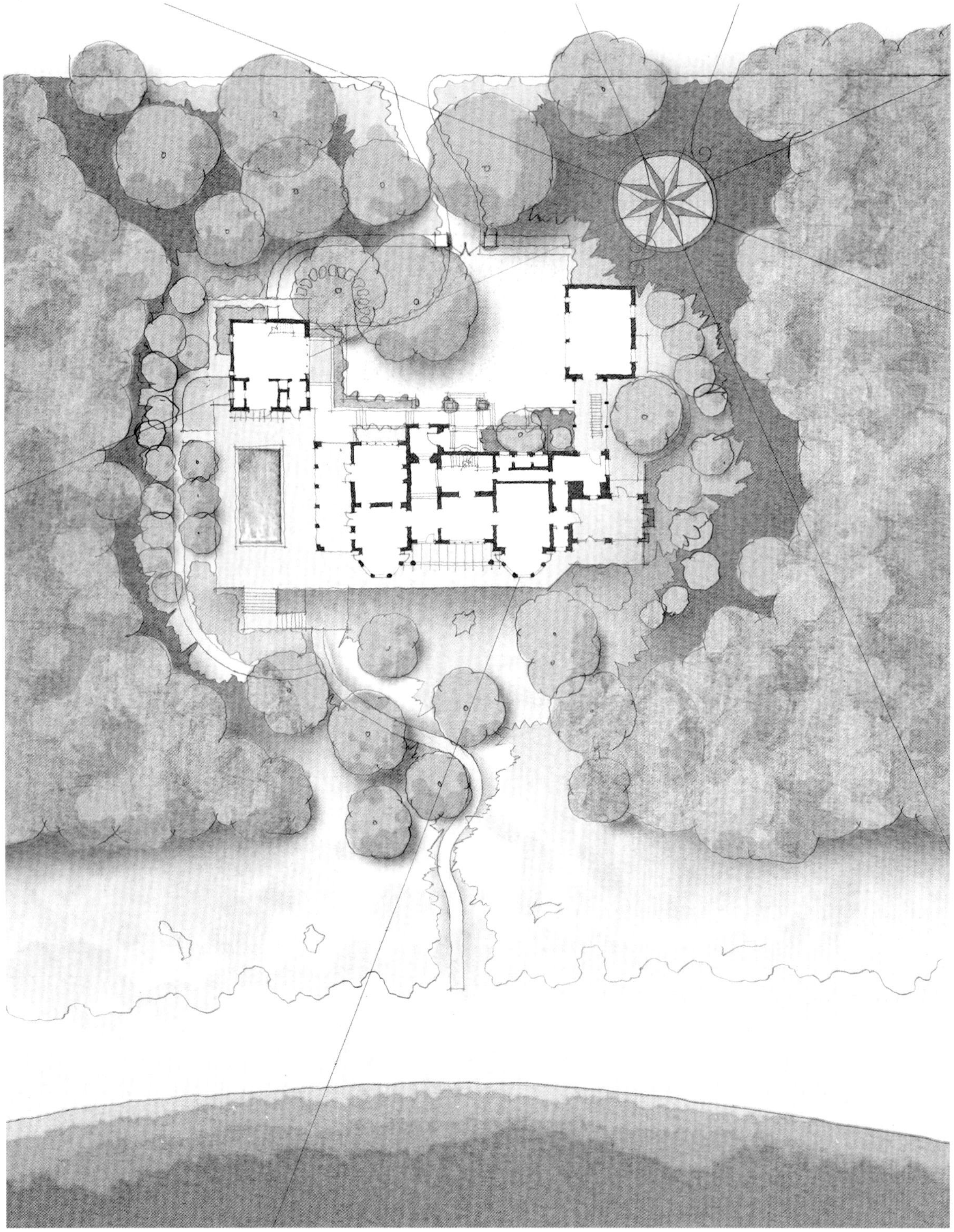

ABOVE AND OVERLEAF: A serpentine boardwalk flanked by native vegetation leads to the dunes and beach beyond. OPPOSITE: Located above the carriage house, a second-story louvered gallery leads to the husband's office.

BOCCE BALL

CHAPTER 10

Mountain Modern

I NEVER IMAGINED that a project in Highlands, North Carolina—a region of the Blue Ridge Mountains characterized by its traditional alpine style—would give me an opportunity to implement the modernist design tenets I studied in school. However, clients with a discerning eye for fine art and contemporary architecture challenged me to do just that: build a home with a distinctive, pared-down aesthetic that was appropriate within the local architectural vernacular. We achieved this by creating a highly personal design, imbued with native materials, that balanced the wife's eye for Bauhaus-esque minimalism with the husband's eye for history and tradition.

The heavily wooded lot created unique challenges. With a deep ravine and active stream on one side of the property and a steep drop-off on the other, buildable space was limited. Our solution was to construct a bridge over the creek, creating an unusual entry sequence. From the street, the house is barely visible, offering only a small peek into the private world that lies beyond. But once guests cross the bridge, through the porte cochere, and into the motor court, they're met with the striking glass wall that is the entrance. A linear L-shaped floor plan was designed along the fairway of an adjacent golf course so that sweeping views of the land were prominent from most of the rooms.

Embracing restraint, we leaned almost exclusively on three exterior building materials: vertical wood board and

PAGE 221: A peek into the living room from the foyer offers insight into the owners' passion for collecting an array of disparate, yet exquisite, decorative objects and art. PREVIOUS SPREAD AND RIGHT: The welcoming glass-front entry is framed by pleached hornbeams. OVERLEAF: Twelve-foot-tall doors unite indoor and outdoor spaces. Board-formed concrete was used for the contemporary fireplaces and chimneys.

board-formed concrete siding for the walls and a standing seam metal roof. The wood siding and metal roof are popular in traditional building methods, but the board-formed concrete (a technique from the brutalist period where molds of wooden boards are cast in concrete) along with the vertical orientation of the boards themselves, give the structure a contemporary edge. We stained the exterior a dark, rich, bark-colored brown to blend into the wooded setting.

Indoors, there is a push-pull of expansive, open spaces contrasted by smaller, more intimate rooms. We wanted to keep the interior material selections as limited as the exterior. Thoughtfully-colored plaster walls and reclaimed wood beams offer an organic variation in texture. The hardwood floors were stained lighter than usual for this area, allowing them to reflect light and blend seamlessly with the reclaimed French limestone in the entry. These elements, combined with the textiles chosen by the designer, create a symphony of warm and cool neutrals.

The biggest decorative anomaly in this house is a top-floor observatory wrapped with windows on three sides. Rising above the treetops, it offers panoramic views of the surrounding landscape. The abundance of color, pattern, and ornamentation creates an unexpected distinction from the rooms downstairs. Ironically, the observatory has become a great sanctuary for our clients to rest, read, and reflect.

There's an undeniable harmony found in the juxtaposition of this structure. This state of equilibrium is what makes the house so peaceful. During the pandemic the clients decided to embrace the tranquility year-round. It's fulfilling knowing our designs afford our clients such a strong sense of solace and belonging.

bauhaus

ABOVE AND RIGHT: This beloved Moroccan-inspired room—referred to as the observatory—is the perfect spot for enjoying the views, bird-watching, or simply having drinks before dinner. With inspiration from the clients and in collaboration with designer Timothy Whealon, we worked to meld the contemporary spaces downstairs with this whimsical and unexpected space upstairs.

North Carolina Architecture

LEFT: The house takes full advantage of the fairway views both inside and out. ABOVE: The bridge traverses the stream to give a sense of distance to the otherwise compact property.

CHAPTER 11

Palladian Hospitality

WHEN THESE CLIENTS came to us for a new house on the North Shore of Chicago—an area rich with early twentieth-century homes designed by some of the city's most noteworthy architects like David Adler and Howard Van Doren Shaw—our utmost concern was creating something that effortlessly blended into the historic neighborhood. In addition, the midwestern couple had always been drawn to the character and hospitality of southern architecture. They decided it was time to leave their downtown Chicago high-rise for the southern-style home they longed for, with a gracious, welcoming presence fit for their growing family.

Through our conversations with the clients, we came up with the idea of combining the southern design sensibilities they were drawn to with Palladian Revival architecture, a style more suited for the neighborhood. The symmetrical pedimented facade features a central round window, modillions, and alluring, scrolled limestone entryway are all attributes of Palladian Revival architecture. The detailed carvings on the limestone entry include local flora as well as a pineapple (a traditional symbol of hospitality). Southern techniques were introduced inside with heart-pine flooring and a central stair hall, enveloped by understated raised paneling that focuses the gaze immediately on the view of the gardens beyond.

A cozy library of rich hemlock paneling boasts a

PAGE 233: The home features a carved Indiana limestone scrolled pediment with fluted pilasters and Corinthian capitals. PREVIOUS SPREAD: Reclaimed limestone piers flank the granite driveway, which leads to a gravel motor court. RIGHT: The residence's door, with its low and wide proportions, draws on Early American design influences.

plethora of architectural details, such as brass rim locks, paneled jambs, operable shutters, and carved moldings. A serene living and dining room showcase the most formal architecture in the house, while the family wing gives way to a more casual approach. The home's two distinct staircases delineate the hierarchy of materials that shifts as one progresses through the home. The front staircase features more refined details, including a custom newel post reflecting Early American architecture, while the back staircase—located in a corridor with rustic brick pavers and board walls—possesses a lighter, more unexpected cutout design.

Inside and out, we made sure to create moments that evoke a passage of time, as if the house had, indeed, been built in the early twentieth century along with the other storied homes of the neighborhood. While the front facade is completely symmetrical, it gives way to a rambling rear facade with contrasting materials and a more informal style. At the rear, clapboard appendages extend from the main brick core of the house, giving the appearance of a past renovation. One contains a light-filled dining area with dramatic floor-to-ceiling windows on three sides, suggesting a porch might have been enclosed at one point. This sun-drenched space facilitates a strong connection to the outdoors year-round.

These moments of authenticity, used in conjunction with period detailing, permitted us to craft a residence that is indistinguishably new, the perfect neighbor to its twentieth-century counterparts.

Painted wood paneling enhances the richness of the architecture. The central archway, which delineates the foyer from the stairwell, is based on one at historic Drayton Hall in South Carolina.

ABOVE AND OPPOSITE: Details from various Early American homes were combined to create this unique stair.

BUNNY WILLIAMS' POINT OF VIEW
The Great Lady Decorators
MAXIMALISM

LEFT: The interiors were created in tandem with designer Suzanne Kasler, who incorporated plush textures and metallic accents in the living room. Contemporary accessories line the bookcases we designed with meticulous millwork. OVERLEAF: The classical dining room features a Gracie hunt-country wallcovering atop a paneled wainscot.

ABOVE AND RIGHT: The library is wrapped in hemlock paneling. The wood's small knots and other characteristics are celebrated for their uniqueness and character. The space has become a favorite of our client.

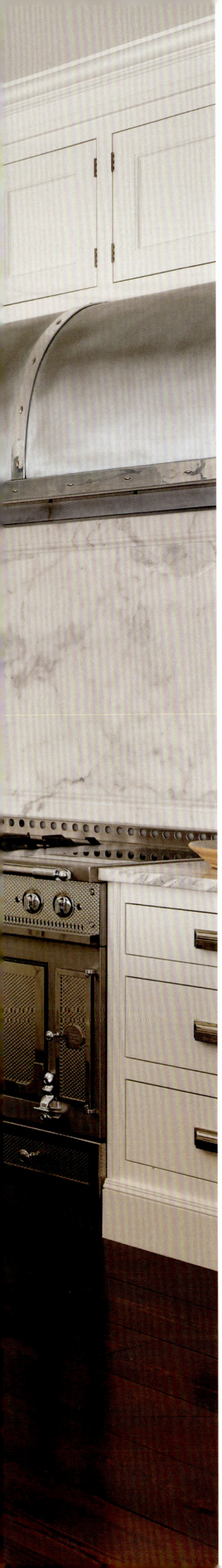

LEFT: A paneled marble backsplash echoes a similar pattern on the island. ABOVE: A cozy nook in the kitchen provides a perch for casual dining or conversing with whomever is cooking.

Connected to the outdoors by floor-to-ceiling windows, the breakfast room is a hub—morning, noon, and night. OVERLEAF: The back entry features brick flooring and a stair railing with a naïve, cutout-wave motif.

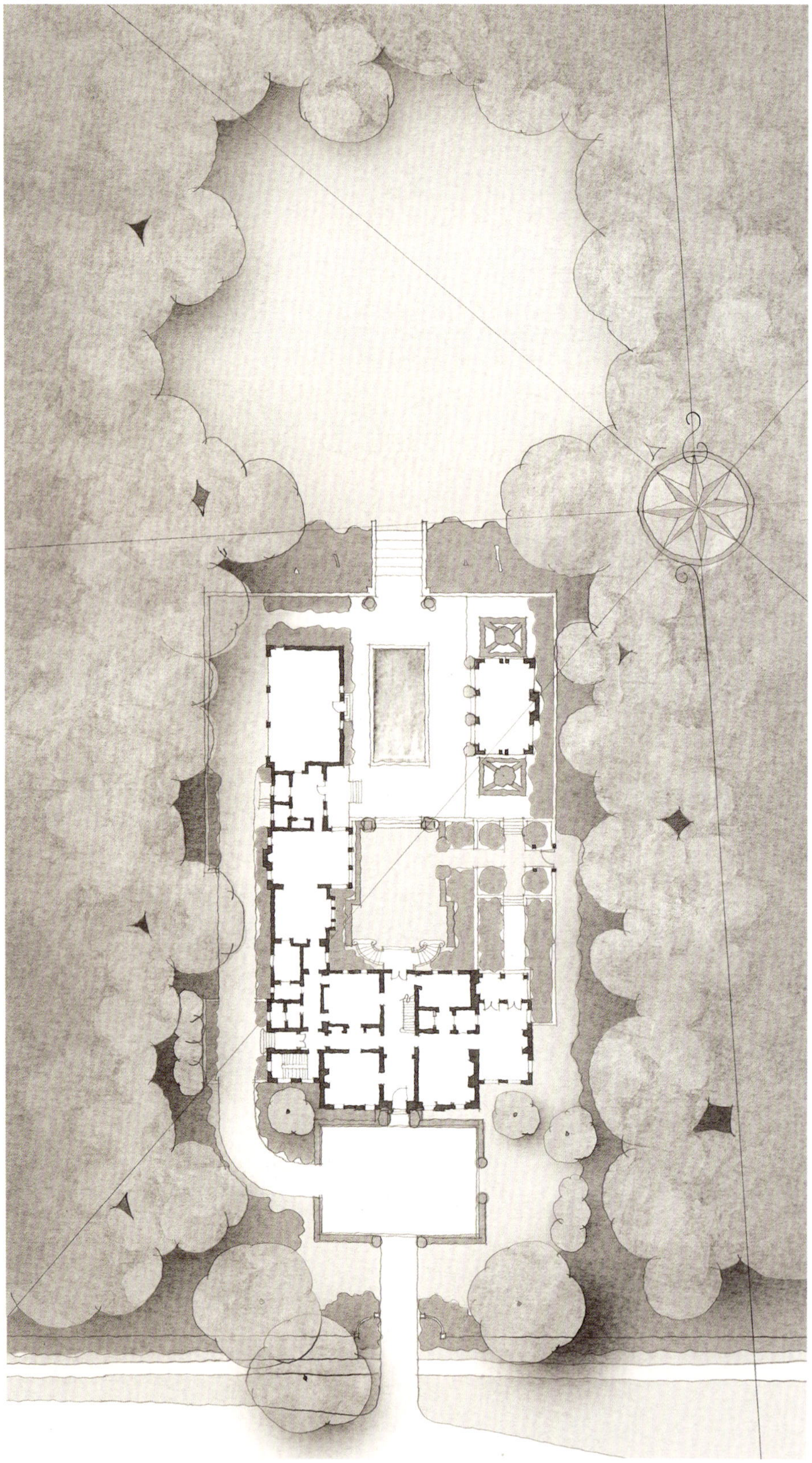

ABOVE: Because the lot is narrow, we designed an L-shaped structure to accommodate gardens, parking, and a pool. RIGHT: The scrolled-iron archway was original but moved to align with the room beyond.

CHAPTER 12

Curated Narrative

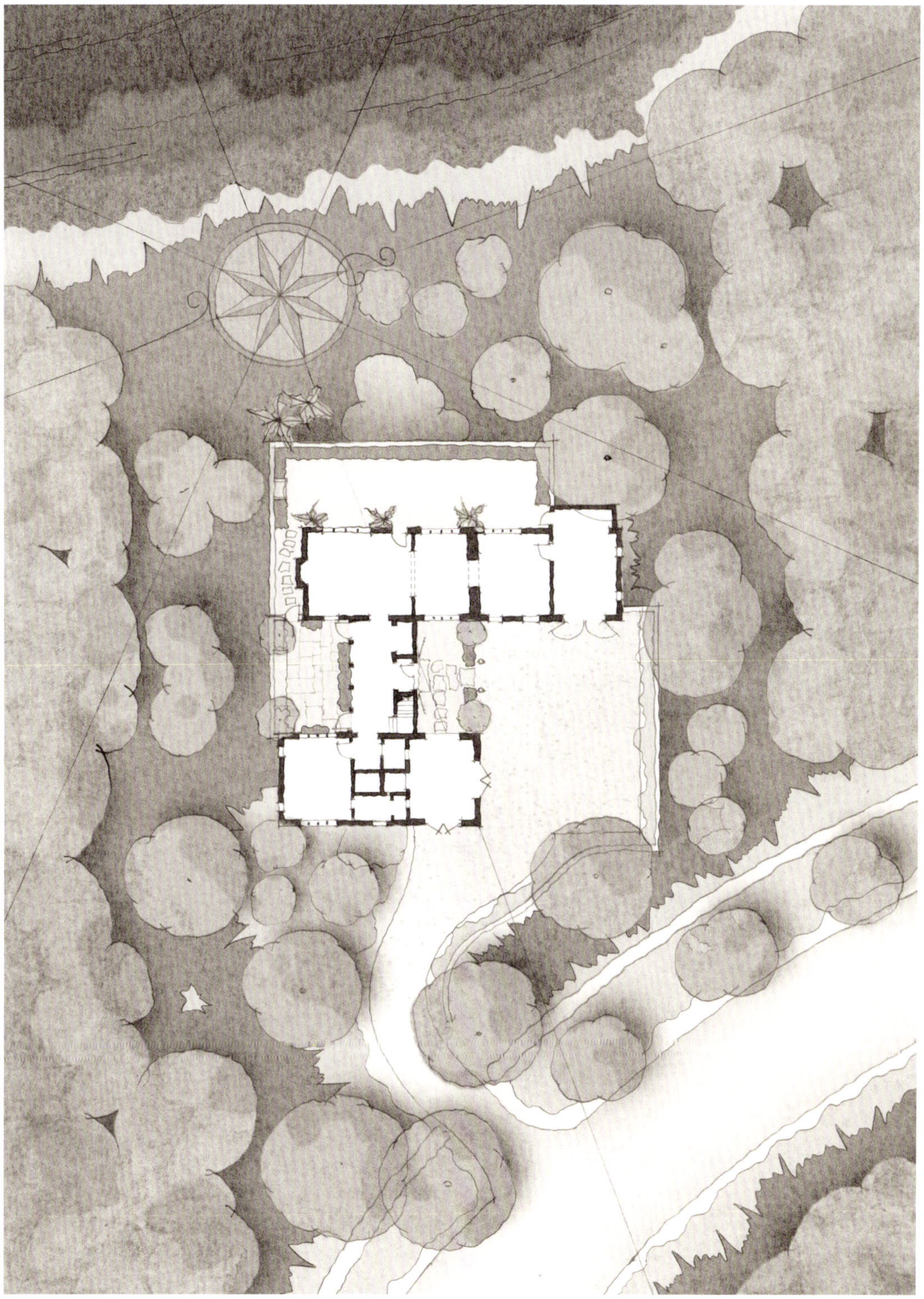

PREVIOUS PAGE: Nestled among indigenous vegetation, our South Carolina island project overlooks a deep-water lagoon. LEFT: The entry portal and louvered shutters were inspired by the Gothic-style arched stable doors of the Aiken-Rhett House in Charleston. ABOVE: The site plan reveals just how intimate the house is, with its natural surroundings purposely juxtaposing the streetscape.

IN ONE OF MY FIRST conversations with the client about designing this new house on Kiawah Island, South Carolina, she mentioned her desire for the house to resemble an abandoned historic structure that we had stumbled upon and refurbished. The client didn't specify a particular type of building she had in mind, but she felt strongly that it should display a patina or nostalgia brought about through architectural vestiges of the past. In short, our task was to build a house that tells a story.

I recommended imagining that we had discovered an old carriage house and renovated it for residential use. Our client found this narrative quite intriguing, and we proceeded to design two stable blocks to feel as though they'd been restored and connected by a new addition that resembles a gallery with floor-to-ceiling windows. This concept made sense for several reasons. First, the layout would blend into the site quite seamlessly. In addition, the Aiken-Rhett House, a nearby estate, set historical precedent for our design, ensuring that our backstory would not come off as random or contrived. We felt strongly that this idea could be executed authentically without falling into cliché. We collectively reflected on this narrative to inform every design decision along the way.

Rather than using overt gestures, we let the materials and finishes do a lot of the work in telling the story. On the main level, dark-gray limestone blocks were placed in a random running band, and upstairs rough-hewn plank floorboards were used—both flooring choices evocative of an old stable. Outside, Gothic Revival arched carriage doors and shutters reference the carriage house at the Aiken-Rhett property and offer a welcoming presence. Masonry exterior walls are finished with a tabby stucco surface embedded with crushed oyster shells, a technique that would have been found on buildings in the region dating back to the 1700s. In some areas we chose to have the tabby walls continue into the interior of the house, reinforcing our story of separate structures having been combined at some point in the past.

What I found most exciting about this project was that it granted me the unique opportunity to create a home for one of my long-time collaborators and friends, designer Jackye Lanham. After twenty years of working on various projects together, developing a vacation home for Jackye and her husband became an inspiring and rewarding exercise for both of us. The process became a laboratory where a rich and intriguing architectural backstory could be melded together with the family's varied collections of beautiful and unique objects. The furnishings carefully chosen by Jackye—compiled from an eclectic mix of English, American, continental, and Anglo-Indian antiques; slipcovered furnishings; and a wide array of art from around the world—came together to complete the narrative. Our open-mindedness and years of experience working together allowed us to push the envelope on many of our design choices, resulting in a truly one-of-a-kind final product—a house that tells a story.

A historic stable would not have had a grand entry door, thus we chose to keep this one understated. It's flanked by an antique lantern on one side and a large shutter on the other.

ABOVE: From the entry, floor-to-ceiling windows offer expansive views into the lush courtyard. OPPOSITE: Portieres flank a wet bar, where guests can help themselves to a drink.

RIGHT: Designer Jackye Lanham assembled a beautiful collection of porcelain, and we created simple, carpenter-style shelving in the dining room to accommodate—and accentuate—pieces on display. OVERLEAF: The living room was designed for maximum comfort and is the prime gathering spot for languorous days. Plaster walls create a cocooning effect and provide a clean backdrop for collections.

ABOVE: Attention to every detail is of utmost importance to the narrative, such as the eighteenth-century hardware adjoining a simple linen closet. RIGHT: The kitchen, designed for efficient functionality, features Gothic-style windows that echo the exterior arches. The island we designed of rustic wood boards is placed on wheels and can be moved as needed.

ABOVE: The husband is an avid collector, reader, and book lover, and his cozy study was designed especially for his personal pursuits as well as a place to work. RIGHT: Exposed conduit in the upstairs gallery gives the impression that electricity was added to the space long after it was originally built. Uneven floorboards offer a glimpse to the downstairs, as they would in an old stable loft that has settled over time.

ABOVE: The guest bedroom, situated within the exposed eaves of the upper floor, offers a quiet escape. OPPOSITE: Decorative fan cutouts top the mirrored doors that lead to a dressing room beyond.

ABOVE AND RIGHT: Artfully incorporated linen cupboards line the vestibule leading to the primary sleeping quarters.

RIGHT: Overscale reclaimed bluestone sets the foundation for the courtyard. With the Lowcountry's temperate climate, the space is ideal for entertaining almost all yearlong. The area is enclosed with a wall of reclaimed Charleston brick, fostering an intimate setting. The sound from the fountain, a twelve-foot-long antique trough sourced in Europe, cultivates tranquility. OVERLEAF: Shadows from the iron gate that we designed for the courtyard shift throughout the day.

CHAPTER 13

Riverfront Revival

THE REMARKABLY unspoiled views of tidal marshes and river vistas from the expansive rear porches of this home on South Carolina's John's Island are spellbinding. The Kiawah River's continuous ebb and flow, nature's emphatic and ephemeral sounds, and endlessly captivating sights, suspend time and lull you into a state of tranquility. Clients from nearby Charleston came to us asking for a new primary residence. They chose John's Island for its natural beauty and proximity to Charleston; this location unites the quiet and privacy of a pastoral landscape with the knowledge that a buzzing city is never too far away.

For this project, we were undeniably inspired by the site and its surrounding landscape, which had been left untouched until now. Accordingly, we took great care and sensitivity in creating structures that honored this special property. The distinguished live oaks guided us in siting the house. We took inspiration from the language of Greek Revival architecture, a vernacular that fits this young family's sensibilities. He wanted something traditional and timeless, yet she made it clear she did not want a house that looked like it was her grandmother's. She wanted something that felt light and suitable to their stage in life.

Greek Revival detailing can be pared down and given a more contemporary feel that works well for a modern family lifestyle of easy, unfussy elegance. The limewashed brick core of the home, flanked by two equally proportioned wood-clad wings, feels genuine to the space as if it was adapted over time. We experimented with the scale of the windows to create an interesting interplay: the central block of the house has fewer, but quite large windows. This strategy gives the home a strong sense of presence, while simultaneously making the overall structure feel less complicated. This play on proportion is subtle, but it is one of the ways in which we were able to infuse tradition with a fresh point of view.

Other distilled, clean-lined features include the octagonal columns capped with a bold capital in the Greek Revival style. These are far less decorative than the classic Corinthian archetype that features heavily detailed acanthus leaves spilling out from a votive basket. Rather than a more formal paved entry, we designed an oyster shell driveway with a grass strip down its center to make it seem as if the grass had been worn down by tractor treads over the course of time.

Inside, we wanted the finishes we selected to feel refined and unexpected. For the floors, we decided on what I call a swept pine finish, a look common in Swedish country houses and historic English manors. The finish feels vintage and helps to refract light throughout the rooms. The staircase, whose newel posts echo the exterior columns, is unique, making it a pleasing focal point. I find this to be one of the most memorable elements of the house.

For these clients, this "old" new home on the river has embraced an active household full of family and friends, striking just the right tone for a gracious and elegant lifestyle. It is a house worthy of the majesty of its environment.

PAGE 281: The enchanting grounds were designed in collaboration with landscape architect Glen Gardner. The carriage house is in the foreground, and the pigeonnier in the distance camouflages the generator. PREVIOUS SPREAD: The property's grand live oaks guided us on how to best site the house. Their majestic size adds a strong sense of belonging and place to this new home. OPPOSITE: The octagonal newel posts on the entry stair recall the octagonal columns on the exterior.

ABOVE: The lavender glass doorknob and brass rim lock evoke a sense of history. OPPOSITE: Interior designer Tammy Connor was our collaborator on this project, and we both shared a vision of blending the past and present. The wet bar, in a welcoming area off the foyer, was fashioned from an antique piece. Artist Raymond Goins painted the mural. Discreet cabinets built into each of the room's four corners conceal essentials for entertaining.

While traveling, I discovered the early nineteenth-century Greek Revival Nero Portoro marble mantel that became the focal point of the living room. In the two entrances to the kitchen, custom Dutch doors were designed to corral the clients' canines in one area or the other.

Bronze doors not only bestow an element of modern design, but also openly frame the river view beyond and allow access to the sweeping rear porch.

DAWN TO DARK
CHEF
IBIZA BOHEMIA
ART HOUSE
THE HISTORY OF SURFING
SURF
OLD HOUSES
TUTANKHAMUN
FRANCIS SULTANA
BEER
HIPHOP RAISED ME
TARANTINO
BIBLIO-STYLE
Supple Leopard
THE INCAL
Lee Radziwill

LEFT, ABOVE, AND OVERLEAF: The library is enveloped in walls of sinker cypress wood, chosen for its natural color and character. The space is a favorite spot for gathering, listening to the clients' album collection, and watching movies.

ANDY WARHOL
Polaroids 1958–1987
SURFING
QUEER CULTURE
GANGSTER RAP

ABOVE AND OPPOSITE: Double islands in the kitchen were devised for both prepping and cooking, as well as for dining. The side walls are all brick, as if the room had been enclosed over time from an existing structure.

ABOVE: Our site plan illustrates the impoundment we created in front of the house, an ever-evolving natural water feature that promotes biodiversity. The property also features a barn for entertaining, a pickleball court, and dock on the river. RIGHT: On the porch, square columns taper to a unique octagonal design at the top. The floors are painted pine. OVERLEAF: The buildings were positioned to take full advantage of the spectacular beauty of its Lowcountry location.

ACKNOWLEDGMENTS

TO MY WIFE, Shannon, who shares my passion for homes and the beauty of domestic life. You have continued to broaden my views, and you bring so much taste, talent, and style to our partnership, which influences both my work and world view—and informs every page of this book. Your support means everything to me. To my children, Emma and Graham, you are my world.

After years in the making, this book has offered me a gift to reflect and to honor everyone who has made the houses within it a reality.

To my remarkable clients. You've made this book possible, and your support has been invaluable. From our first meetings through planning and construction, each of you has welcomed us with open arms throughout the entire process. And when it came to photography, you graciously invited us back, time and again, from before sunrise until after sunset, to capture the light and attempt to illustrate every design decision that we take into consideration when designing a home for all of life's most personal moments—morning, noon, and night. I cannot thank you enough for supporting our firm's vision and for being the very best of collaborators. I look forward to our next project!

I send the greatest appreciation to these collaborators: Eric Piasecki, photographer (and the ultimate light catcher). Every single image was shot with a passion for beauty and for capturing the essence of each location. Helen Crowther, whether in South Florida or the mountains of North Carolina, your style and taste, along with intuitive sense of place, created magic everywhere we went. Mary Shanahan, our beloved book designer, who always knows how to marry our words and photographs in the most informative and elegant way. Jill Cohen, our agent and adviser. Thank you for your friendship and guidance along with your colleagues, including Lizzy Hyland. More importantly, your enthusiasm and faith in me has elevated my dream. Kathleen Jayes, our Rizzoli editor. Your keen insight, appreciation for printed works, and exquisite eye for detail for the finished book will not soon be forgotten. Clinton Smith, our collaborator on the book's text. Thank you for listening, as well as reading between the lines, to create a manuscript and captions that beautifully inform our project's photographs. Emmaline Dixon, a creative confidante. You've offered a fresh insight into our firm's work and point of view. Beth Lang, sister. Thank you for everything. Thank you to friends Kevin O'Gara and Denise Wilbert for your helpful hands throughout the project. Charlotte Moss, designer and author. Your foreword reinforces my notion of hard work and my never-ending love of houses and home. Charles Miers, publisher of Rizzoli. You believed in our work early on—thank you for the support and the encouragement to get going with it.

To colleagues past and present, your contributions have been invaluable to the creation of this book. No house is created in isolation, and I'm forever grateful for my teams of collaborators over the years: the builders, landscape architects, interior designers, craftsmen, artisans, and vendors who helped to bring these houses to life.

To my outrageously talented team whose camaraderie and compassion for each other coalesces every single day to create the most collaborative office culture, of which our clients are the beneficiaries of your combined creativity. I want to thank the current and former project architects and staff members whose expertise also played a significant part in the creation of this book: especially Jacques Levet, a beautiful talent within our office who graciously and enthusiastically rendered each site plan to be both artistic and informative; Ashley Abballe, Callie Beal, Steve Fintak, Patrick Hannon, Karen Hodgdon, McLean Jenkins, Peter Klein, Nate Neiers, Rene Salas, Chad Sardi, Claire Smith, Robert Smith, Clark Templeton, Shannon Dixon, Ashlea Biggers, Mary O'Gara, Bill Davis, Syl Bartos, Cameron Bishop, Emmaline Dixon, Rachel Edrington, Mike Hoenes, Jonathan LaCrosse, Sarah Malaby, Christine Neptune, Katie Pope, Kyle Taylor.

PROJECT CREDITS

CHAPTER 1: NEOCLASSICAL ELEGANCE
Clark Templeton, project architect
Carolyn Malone Interiors, interior design
Howard Design Studio, landscape architect
Breiding Construction, builder

CHAPTER 2: VERNACULAR BARN
Karen Hodgdon, project architect
Barry Dixon, interior design
JW Underwood Construction, builder

CHAPTER 3: ENGLISH ESTATE
Syl Bartos, project manager
Susanne Kasler Interiors, interior design
Howard Design Studio, landscape architect
Chris Conley Homes, Inc., builder

CHAPTER 4: TROPICAL OASIS
Steve Fintak, project architect
Shannon Dixon, interior design
Dee Rennebaum, landscape architect
Worth Builders, Dave Chesser, builder

CHAPTER 5: EDITED STYLE
Cameron Bishop, project manager
Carolyn Malone Interiors, interior design
Gardenology, landscape design
Mike Helenbrook, builder

CHAPTER 6: ISLAND RETREAT
Claire Smith, project manager
Kristen Blood, interior design
The Vine, landscape architect
Russell White Construction, builder

CHAPTER 7: COTSWOLD MANOR
Syl Bartos, project manager
Jacquelynne P. Lanham Designs, Inc., interior design
Howard Design Studio, landscape architect
McGarrity Garcia Custom Builders, builder

CHAPTER 8: LOWCOUNTRY CHARM
Patrick Hannon, project manager
Jacquelynne P. Lanham Designs, Inc., interior design
Solaris, Inc., builder

CHAPTER 9: COASTAL ARTS AND CRAFTS
Clark Templeton, project architect
Beth Webb Interiors, interior design
Glen R. Gardner, Landscape Architect, landscape architect
Russ Cooper Associates, builder

CHAPTER 10: MOUNTAIN MODERN
Claire Smith, project manager
Timothy Whealon Interiors, interior design
JM Landscapes, landscape architect
JW Underwood Construction, builder

CHAPTER 11: PALLADIAN HOSPITALITY
Jonathan LaCrosse and Ashley Abballe, project managers
Suzanne Kasler Interiors, interior design
Mariani Landscape, landscape design
Red Rock Custom Homes, builder

CHAPTER 12: CURATED NARRATIVE
Syl Bastos, project manager
Jacquelynne P. Lanham Designs, Inc., interior design
Glen R. Gardner, Landscape Architect, landscape architect
Solaris, Inc., builder

CHAPTER 13: RIVERFRONT REVIVAL
Cameron Bishop, project manager
Tammy Connor Interior Design, interior design
Glen R. Gardner, Landscape Architect, landscape architect
Sheppard Construction, builder

First published in the United States of America in 2023 by
Rizzoli International Publications, Inc.
49 West 27th Street
New York, NY 10001
www.rizzoliusa.com

Foreword: Charlotte Moss
Text: Clinton Smith
All photography by Eric Piasecki except:
Pages 5, 8: Emily Followill

Publisher: Charles Miers
Senior Editor: Kathleen Jayes
Production Manager: Kaija Markoe
Managing Editor: Lynn Scrabis

Design: Mary Shanahan and Agnethe Glatved
Editorial Production: Vincent Spina

Developed in collaboration with Jill Cohen Associates, LLC.

Printed in Hong Kong

2026 2027 2028 / 10 9 8 7 6 5

ISBN: 978-0-8478-7348-7

Library of Congress Control Number: 2023934730

Visit us online:
Instagram.com/RizzoliBooks
Facebook.com/RizzoliNewYork
Youtube.com/user/RizzoliNY

The authorized representative in the EU for product safety and compliance is Mondadori Libri S.p.A.
via Gian Battista Vico, 42, 20123 Milan, Italy
www.mondadori.it

FSC
www.fsc.org
MIX
Paper | Supporting responsible forestry
FSC™ C023053